There were bodies everywhere. Skeletons, to be exact. They were scattered all over Hardin, Missouri.

The Crisis

The Missouri River had overflowed its banks. The waters swept through Hardin, destroying homes and buildings—and digging up the dead.

The Horror

The local cemetery was in ruins. The flood had unearthed nearly 600 coffins. Thousands of bones littered the small town.

The Experts

Someone had to identify the corpses. But first they had to be put back together again. The town brought in a team of forensic anthropologists. They are experts at identifying human remains.

The Question

What would it take to get the
remains back in their proper graves?
And why did it matter, anyway?

Book Design: Red Herring Design/NYC **Photo Credits:** Photographs © 2012: Alamy Images: 26 background (Deco), 40 right (JG Photography); AP Images: 4, 5 (Tony Gutierrez), 1, 2, 3 (Charlie Riedel), 41 top left (Paul Sancya), 14 (Matt Slocum); Armed Forces Institute of Pathology: 38; Disaster Mortuary Operational Response Team/Paul Sledzik: 21, 22; Getty Images: 32 (Dominic Dibbs), cover bottom (Aaron Graubart), 10 foreground (MedicalRF.com), 18 top (Jeff J. Mitchell), 18 bottom (Oli Scarff); Media Bakery: back cover foreground (Steve Weisbauer), 26 bottom, 36; Paul Sledzik: 29; Peter Arnold Inc./Jim Wark: 13; Peter Brown: 31; Photo Researchers, NY: 40 top (Mauro Fermariello), 40 center (Pascal Goetgheluck), 42, 43 (Roger Harris), 41 top right (David Hay Jones/SPL), 37 (Russell Kightley), 40 left (Peter Skinner); Reuters: 24, 34 (Tomas Bravo), 44, 45; ShutterStock, Inc.: cover background, back cover background, 10 background (Jaimaa), 25 (D. & K. Kucharska), 30 (Mopic), cover top (Pangfolio.com), 8 (Pokaz); Terrie Winson: 41 bottom. Maps by David Lindroth, Inc.

Library of Congress Cataloging-in-Publication Data
Denega, Danielle.
Dead men floating : a small town is awash in skeletons / Danielle Denega.
p. cm.
Includes bibliographical references and index.
ISBN-13 978-0-545-32802-9
ISBN-10 0-545-32802-0
1. Forensic anthropology—Missouri. 2. Human remains
(Archaeology)—Missouri. 3. Floods—Missouri—History. I. Title.
GN69.8.D457 2011
599.909778—dc22
2011003025

DEAD MEN FLOATING

A Small Town Is Awash in Skeletons

DANIELLE DENEGA

TABLE OF CONTENTS

PREVIEW.................1

CHAPTER 1
A Natural Disaster.............10
At first the rain is a nuisance. Then it becomes a nightmare.

CHAPTER 2
Corpses on the Streets................14
A flood is coming—and there is nothing anyone can do to stop it.

Map........................17

CHAPTER 3
Bringing the Dead to Life.....18
Experts try to get a picture of the bodies from the cemetery.

Bone Detective........24

CHAPTER 4
Close-Up on Corpses............26
Forensic experts begin to sort and study the remains.

Skull & Bones...........30

CHAPTER 5
Putting the Pieces Together...........32
Hardin's dead can rest in peace again.

XFILES....................37

ID Expert................38

Body Scan...............40

Bare Bones..............42

1

A Natural Disaster

**At first the rain is a nuisance.
Then it becomes a nightmare.**

When the rain started falling in the spring of 1993, no one could have imagined the devastation it would bring. As storm after storm pummeled the midwestern United States, rivers began to overflow their banks. Throughout the summer, floodwaters destroyed homes and businesses. Roads and bridges were washed away.

The flooding didn't end until the fall. By then, more than 500 counties in nine midwestern states had been hit hard. Floodwaters covered more than 20 million acres (8 million hectares) of land.

Home Wrecker

The wreckage from the flood was terrible. Fifty people died, and 55,000 homes were damaged or destroyed. The flood caused more than $15 billion in damage. Much of the Midwest was declared a disaster area.

The event became known as the Great Flood of 1993. It was one of the worst natural disasters in American history. And the horrors it unleashed would forever haunt one small Missouri town.

HIGHWAY 40 in Missouri was completely underwater when the Missouri River flooded in 1993.

HIGHWAY 40

2

Corpses on the Streets

**A flood is coming—
and there is nothing anyone
can do to stop it.**

Hardin is only six miles (ten kilometers) north of the
Missouri River. So people there knew that it was only
a matter of time before the flood reached their town.

That horrible day came in July 1993. The rushing
waters swept through Hardin, destroying homes and
other buildings. Then something so terrible happened
that the town would never be the same.

The dead rose up from the cemetery.

At the time, there was a small cemetery in Hardin. It had been built in a low-lying area in 1828. It was where most of the town's approximately 600 residents buried their dead.

Digging up the Dead

When the flood hit, water rushed into Hardin Cemetery. It poured into the graves and dug up the coffins. Hundreds of headstones, burial vaults, and coffins were swept away. About half of the 1,576 graves in the cemetery were destroyed.

Even worse, hundreds of coffins broke open. Human remains spilled out and floated through the streets and fields. Some ended up as far as 18 miles (29 km) away.

The people of Hardin were powerless to stop the raging flood and the destruction of the cemetery. They watched in horror as water tore apart the bodies of their loved ones. "People are just heartsick," one resident said to a reporter.

HARDIN, MISSOURI, is located six miles north of the Missouri River.

Hardin, Missouri

The Missouri River overflowed its banks in the Great Flood of 1993. The flood left much of the Midwest under water.

3

Bringing the Dead to Life

Experts try to get a picture of the bodies from the cemetery.

It was like a scene from a horror movie. Some of the corpses in Hardin were fresh and whole. Others had been buried more than a century before. Those remains had broken apart and scattered across town.

The people of Hardin needed help. So they turned to Dean Snow, the county coroner. They wanted him to identify the remains so their loved ones could be laid to rest once more.

Snow organized a special team. It was made up of members of DMORT, or the Disaster Mortuary Operational Response Team. That's a team of experts put together by the U.S. government to help identify bodies after major accidents.

Snow's team included forensic anthropologists. Those are scientists who help identify human remains. The team also included forensic pathologists. Those are medical experts who figure out how a person died.

The team members' mission was clear. They had to find and identify the remains from the cemetery.

Searching for Remains

The first step was to search for these remains. With the help of volunteers from Hardin, team members found nearly 600 coffins. They recovered 3,400 bones, including 129 skulls. They stored the remains in barns and refrigerated trucks at the county fairgrounds.

Next, the team created antemortem profiles of the missing dead. *Antemortem* means "before death." The profiles included information gathered about the people before they died, such as dental and medical

A MEMBER OF the Disaster Mortuary Operational Response Team views the destruction at Hardin Cemetery during the 1993 flood.

records. These records could help the team match identities to remains. For example, if an antemortem profile showed that a person had once broken his leg, the experts would look for a skeleton with that injury.

There was just one problem. For many of the missing dead, dental and medical records weren't available.

Paul Sledzik was a forensic anthropologist from the DMORT team. "In the Hardin disaster," Sledzik explained, "many of the missing had been dead for a very long time."

Dearly Departed

Investigators tried to fill in the gaps. They asked people to describe their missing relatives. Did the dead have any broken bones? What clothes had they been buried in?

Their answers helped the investigators create antemortem profiles for most of the people who had been buried in the cemetery.

The corpses and bones were next.

ANTHROPOLOGISTS EXAMINE pelvic bones collected from Hardin Cemetery after the flood.

Bone Detective

Here's a step-by-step guide to how a forensic anthropologist matches bones to a missing person.

1. Clean the bones.
Use flesh-eating beetles to remove any flesh on the bones. If there's a rush, boil the bones in soapy water instead.

2. Confirm that the bones are human.
Anthropologists can tell the difference between the bones of a human and another animal.

3. Identify the bones.
Decide what part of the body each bone came from. Then "side" the bones—figure out whether the bone came from the left or right side of the body. Finally, lay the bones out the way they would appear if the skeleton were intact.

4. Examine the bones.
Measure, weigh, and x-ray the bones. Study them under a microscope.

5. Create a postmortem profile.
Postmortem means "after death." By examining just a few bones, experts can determine a dead person's age, height, race, and gender. Bones can also reveal how long the person has been dead and what may have caused the death.

6. Compare the profile to the antemortem records.
Look at the missing person's medical records. Do the details match the postmortem profile?

4

Close-Up on Corpses

Forensic experts begin to sort and study the remains.

The DMORT team had finished the antemortem profiles. Now it was time to create postmortem profiles. *Postmortem* means "after death." These postmortem profiles were records of what the team had learned about the corpses and bones.

Team members would then compare the postmortem profiles to the antemortem profiles and try to find matches. That way, they could identify the corpses.

The remains were in various states of decay. Some were new and well preserved. Some were dried up like mummies. Some were skeletons. Others were just pieces of bones. A forensic pathologist handled the bodies that had a lot of soft tissue left. The anthropology team handled the remains that were mostly bones.

Inside the Coffins

Thirty-five of the coffins held complete skeletons. The anthropologists measured the skulls and the long bones. (Those are bones that are longer than they are wide and are rounded at both ends.)

Personal items, such as watches or blankets, were often found inside the coffins. That information was added to the postmortem profiles.

Some bodies had been torn from their coffins. Sledzik and the others did what they could to create profiles of these skeletons. They measured bones to discover a person's age, race, gender, and height. The anthropologists also looked for evidence of broken bones or diseases. But these were the easy cases. Others would turn out to be more difficult—and gruesome.

SKULLS ARE LINED UP at the morgue set up outside Hardin.

Skull & Bones

The skeleton is the bony framework of the body. When people are born, they have more than 300 bones. As they grow, some of those bones join together. Adults have only about 206 bones.

Human Skeleton

- cranium
- mandible
- clavicle
- humerus
- scapula
- sternum
- rib
- radius
- vertebra
- ulna
- hip
- sacrum
- carpals
- coccyx
- metacarpals
- phalanges
- femur
- patella
- tibia
- fibula
- tarsals
- metatarsals

The cranium, or upper part of the skull, holds and protects the brain. Eight bony plates form the human cranium. They fit together at joints called sutures. The human head also includes 14 facial bones that form the lower front of the skull. They provide the framework for most of the face.

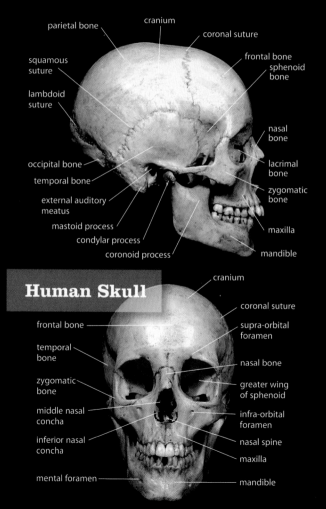

parietal bone

cranium

coronal suture

squamous suture

frontal bone

sphenoid bone

lambdoid suture

nasal bone

occipital bone

lacrimal bone

temporal bone

zygomatic bone

external auditory meatus

mastoid process

condylar process

maxilla

coronoid process

mandible

Human Skull

cranium

coronal suture

frontal bone

supra-orbital foramen

temporal bone

zygomatic bone

nasal bone

greater wing of sphenoid

middle nasal concha

infra-orbital foramen

inferior nasal concha

nasal spine

mental foramen

maxilla

mandible

5

Putting the Pieces Together

Hardin's dead can rest in peace again.

Paul Sledzik and his team continued their work on the postmortem profiles. They turned to the hundreds of loose bones they had found. All of the bits and pieces had to be sorted.

The forensic anthropologists sorted the bones by type. They put skulls in one place. Tibias—bones found in the shins—were put in another area. Femurs—thighbones—were grouped together, and so on.

A FORENSIC ANTHROPOLOGIST
pieces together a human skeleton

After sorting the bones, the anthropologists tried to "side" them. That's the process of figuring out whether a bone is from the left or right side of the body.

Next, the experts grouped the bones according to age. Finally, they tried to separate males from females.

The team found it nearly impossible to put together whole skeletons. However, they were able to estimate the number of people whose remains they found. The flood had washed away the remains of 793 people. The team estimated that they had found about 600 of these bodies.

Personal Profiles

As the team members finished examining the remains, they moved on to their final task. They compared the postmortem profiles to the antemortem profiles. Slowly, they began to identify bodies.

Some cases were easy to solve. A well-preserved body might be identified by a tattoo. A coffin could be linked to a name by a piece of jewelry found inside.

In the end, Sledzik and the rest of the DMORT team identified the remains of 119 people.

By October 1993, the DMORT team had left town. The people of Hardin prepared to rebury the remains that could not be identified. Bones and pieces of bones were placed in 476 separate vaults. Each vault was carefully tagged so it could be linked with its postmortem profile.

Vernie Fountain led a team of funeral directors who helped respond to the disaster. He told the *New York Times* that the flood had been terrible for the families of the missing dead. "You bury someone and you expect them to be buried for eternity," he said. ✘

ID EXPERT 38

BODY SCAN............................ 40

BARE BONES 42

RESOURCES 44

GLOSSARY 46

INDEX 48

FILES

ID Expert

Forensic anthropologist Paul Sledzik identifies the dead for a living.

PAUL SLEDZIK works for the National Transportation Safety Board in Washington, D.C.

How did you become interested in anthropology?

SLEDZIK: I had always had an interest in biology, history, archeology, and human evolution. Then I had a really interesting anthropology professor. I was hooked.

How did you get into the forensic side of anthropology?

SLEDZIK: I did a few forensic cases with the college professor I liked. But most of my forensic experience came from the Armed Forces Institute of Pathology. That's where I learned the techniques and applications of the field.

What does a forensic anthropologist do?

SLEDZIK: Most forensic anthropologists work on individual skeletal cases. I tend to look at disaster situations. I make sure different agencies work together to identify victims of disasters. I work with family members, federal government officials, and scientists.

How is forensic anthropology useful in large disasters?

SLEDZIK: First, forensic anthropologists identify remains. Second, they help with the search and recovery. Third, they help manage the overall identification efforts.

What questions do you ask at a mass disaster site?

SLEDZIK: Are you dealing with whole bodies or parts of bodies? Are the bodies spread over a large area or in a small site? Is it a closed population disaster? (Plane crashes are a closed population disaster because you know how many people were on the plane.) Or is it an open population disaster—and you don't know how many people were involved?

Is it hard to work with family members of the victims?

SLEDZIK: Loved ones have to provide us with a lot of information. We, in turn, need to keep them informed about what's going on.

Are there other challenges?

SLEDZIK: Sure. We have to get antemortem information to make an identification. In cases like Hurricane Katrina, records were flooded. So the information wasn't available.

What advice would you give students who are interested in forensic anthropology?

SLEDZIK: Figure out what you really like about forensic science. Many TV shows portray it in a glamorous way. In reality it's a lot of lab work. You aren't working with criminals. You're working with information and data and samples. So, if it's the glamour that you're after, it may not be for you!

What part of your job do you enjoy the most?

SLEDZIK: I like not knowing what will happen day to day. There could be an accident in the next hour that I have to go out to. Or I could get a call from a family member with a unique question. Or there could be a call from a medical examiner with information about a new aspect of victim identification.

Body Scan

Check out a forensic anthropologist's tools of the trade.

1 Caliper: This tool is used to measure the size of bones.

2 Microscope: Anthropologists sometimes have to look for details that can't be seen with the naked eye.

3 FORDISC 3.0 software: Anthropologists use this program to help determine the race and gender of a skull. They type in 21 measurements from a skull. The computer does the rest.

4 X-ray machine: This device uses high-energy beams to create images of teeth, bones, and organs inside the body.

5 Clay, wig, prosthetic eyes: Forensic anthropologists use these when they do facial reconstruction on a human skull.

6 Osteometric board: This tool is used to find the lengths of the long bones of a skeleton.

7 Latex gloves: Anthropologists wear protective gloves when they handle evidence.

8 Tyvek suit: Anthropologists wear this suit when they work with remains. It protects against dangerous germs. Tyvek is nearly impossible to tear. It allows only water vapor to pass through.

Bare Bones

Here's how forensic anthropologists get information from bones.

6 Gender: Males tend to have narrower pelvic bones than females. A female pelvis is wider to allow for childbirth.

7 Age: If the front of the pelvic bone is bumped or ridged, the person was young. Older people have smoother pelvic bones.

8 Age: Teenagers have femurs (thighbones) that are knobby.

9 Age: Older adults may have signs of arthritis at the joints.

male

female

1 Gender: Male jaws tend to be square. Female jaws are more pointed.

2 Race: Anthropologists can get clues about a person's race from the length of the jaw, the distance between the eyes, the openings in the nose, and the slant of the cheekbones.

3 Is it human? Are the back teeth dull and the front teeth sharper? If so, they belonged to a human.

4 Age: Small children have baby teeth. Older children have permanent teeth. In older adults the teeth may be worn down.

5 Occupation: When muscles get heavy use, bony ridges form where the muscle attaches to the bone. People who worked with their hands might have noticeable ridges on the bones of their wrists.

Here's a selection of books and websites for more information about forensic anthropology.

What to Read Next

NONFICTION

Bass, Bill, and Jon Jefferson. *Death's Acre: Inside the Legendary Forensic Lab—the Body Farm—Where the Dead Do Tell Tales.* New York: Putnam, 2003.

Benedict, Jeff. *No Bone Unturned: The Adventures of a Top Smithsonian Forensic Scientist and the Legal Battle for America's Oldest Skeletons.* New York: HarperCollins, 2003.

Denega, Danielle. *Skulls and Skeletons: True-Life Stories of Bone Detectives.* New York: Franklin Watts, 2007.

Hopping, Lorraine Jean. *Bone Detective: The Story of Forensic Anthropologist Diane France.* Washington, D.C.: Joseph Henry Press, 2006.

Platt, Richard. *Crime Scene: The Ultimate Guide to Forensic Science.* New York: DK Publishing, 2003.

Shone, Rob. *Corpses and Skeletons: The Science of Forensic Anthropology.* New York: Rosen Publishing, 2008.

Thomas, Peggy. *Forensic Anthropology: The Growing Science of Talking Bones.* New York: Facts On File, 2003.

Yancey, Diane. *Body Farms.* Detroit: Lucent Books, 2009.

FICTION

Grisham, John. *Theodore Boone: Kid Lawyer.* New York: Dutton, 2010.

Websites

American Anthropological Association
http://www.aaanet.org/index.htm

The AAA promotes the science of anthropology. Check out the "For Students" page under the Resources tab.

American Board of Forensic Anthropology
http://www.theabfa.org

The ABFA certifies forensic anthropologists and has advice for students interested in the field.

ForensicAnthro.com
http://www.forensicanthro.com

This website provides information about forensic anthropology.

History Detectives
http://www.pbs.org/opb/historydetectives/techniques/forensic.html

Learn how forensic techniques play a major role in "history sleuthing."

UT Knoxville Forensic Anthropology Center
http://web.utk.edu/~fac

This is the website of the University of Tennessee's Forensic Anthropology Center.

Young Forensic Scientists Forum
http://www2.aafs.org/yfsf

This site helps educate young people who are interested in working in forensics.

GLOSSARY

antemortem (an-tee-MORE-tuhm) *adjective* before death

anthropology (an-thruh-POL-uh-jee) *noun* the study of human beings, including their bones, language, and culture

arthritis (ar-THRY-tis) *noun* a disease that causes sore, inflamed, or stiffened joints

cemetery (SEM-uh-teh-ree) *noun* a place where people are buried after they die

corpse (KORPS) *noun* a dead human body

cranium (KRAY-nee-uhm) *noun* another word for *skull*, especially the part that covers the brain

decay (di-KAY) *noun* the breaking down of plant or animal matter by natural causes

devastation (dev–uh-STAY-shun) *noun* severe damage or destruction

DMORT (DEE-mort) *noun* a team of experts who help identify victims and prepare them for burial after big disasters or accidents; DMORT stands for *Disaster Mortuary Operational Response Team*

evidence (EV-uh-denss) *noun* materials gathered during an investigation that provide clues

expert (EKS-purt) *noun* a person who has knowledge and experience in a certain field

femur (FEE-mur) *noun* the thighbone

forensic anthropologist (fuh-REN-sik an-thruh-POL-uh-jist) *noun* a scientist who studies bones and uses that knowledge in investigations

forensic anthropology (fuh-REN-sik an-thruh-POL-uh-jee) *noun* the study and use of bone knowledge in investigations

forensic pathologist (fuh-REN-sik path-OL-uh-jist) *noun* a medical expert who determines the official cause and manner of death

gender (JEN-dur) *noun* the sex of a person or other animal

identify (eye-DEN-tuh-fye) *verb* to establish who someone is or what something is

joint (JOINT) *noun* a place where two bones meet

long bone (LONG BONE) *noun* a bone that has a long shaft and knobs on both ends

microscope (MYE-kruh-skope) *noun* a tool that makes objects appear larger so they can be studied

pelvic bone (PEL-vik BONE) *noun* a hip bone

postmortem (pohst-MORE-tuhm) *adjective* after death

pummel (PUHM-uhl) *verb* to strike something or someone repeatedly

remains (ri-MAYNZ) *noun* dead bodies

skeleton (SKEL-uh-tuhn) *noun* the bony framework of the body

skull (SKUHL) *noun* the bony frame of the head

sutures (SOO-churz) *noun* joints that hold the bones of the skull together

tibia (TIH-bee-uh) *noun* one of the two bones in the shin

tissue (TISH-oo) *noun* a fabric of the same kind of cells. There are four main kinds: muscles, tissue made up of muscle cells; epithelial tissue, which covers the surface of the body; connective tissue, which helps support and join together parts of the body; and nervous tissue, which carries nerve signals throughout the body.

unearth (uhn-URTH) *verb* to dig up

vault (VAWLT) *noun* an underground burial chamber

x-ray (EKS-ray) *verb* to photograph a body part with radiation, which allows doctors and scientists to see through skin

INDEX

age, 25, 28, 35, 42
animal bones, 25, 43
antemortem profiles, 20, 23, 25, 27, 35, 39
Armed Forces Institute of Pathology, 38

bones, 20, *22*, 23, *24*, 25, *26*, 27–28, *29*, *30–31*, 33, *34*, 35, 36, 40, 41, *41*, *42–43*

calipers, 40, *40*
cemetery. *See* Hardin Cemetery.
clay, 41, *41*
closed population disasters, 39
coffins, 16, 20, 28, *32*, 35
computers, 40, *40*
coroner, 19
corpses, 16, 19, 23, 27–28

damage, 11, 12, 15, 16
decay, 28
dental records, 20, 23
Disaster Mortuary Operational Response Team (DMORT), 20, *21*, *22*, 23, 27, 28, 33, 35, 36

facial bones, 31, *31*
facial reconstructions, 41, *41*
family members, 16, 19, 23, 38, 39
flesh-eating beetles, 25
flood. *See* Great Flood of 1993.
FORDISC 3.0 software, 40, *40*
forensic anthropologists, 20, *22*, 23, *24*, 25, 28, 33, *34*, 35, 38–39, *38*, 40–41, 42–43
forensic pathologists, 20, 28
Fountain, Vernie, 36
funeral directors, 36

gender, 25, 28, 35, 40, 42, 43
germs, 41
graves, 16
Great Flood of 1993, 11–12, *13*, *14*, 15, 16, *17*, *18*, *21*, 36

Hardin Cemetery, *14*, 16, 20, *21*, *22*, 23

Hardin, Missouri, *14*, 15–16, *17*, 19, 20, *21*, *22*, 23, *29*, 33, 36
Hurricane Katrina, 39

identification, 19, 20, 23, 25, 27–28, 35, 36, 38, 39

latex gloves, 41, *41*

map, *17*
medical records, 20, 23, 25, 39
microscopes, 25, 40, *40*
Missouri River, *13*, 15, *17*

news reports, 16, 36

occupations, 43
open population disasters, 39
osteometric boards, 41, *41*

personal items, 23, 28, 35
postmortem profiles, 25, 27, 28, 33, 35, 36
prosthetic eyes, 41, *41*

race, 25, 28, 40, 43
remains, 16, 19, 20, 23, 27, 28, 35-36, 39, 41
reconstructions, 25, 41, *41*

"siding," 25, 35
skulls, 20, *24*, *26*, 28, *29*, *31*, 33, 40, 41
Sledzik, Paul, 23, 28, 33, 35, 38–39, *38*
Snow, Dean, 19–20
sorting, 33, *34*, 35
storms, 11, 39
sutures, 31

tools, 40–41, *40*, *41*
Tyvek suits, 41, *41*

vaults, 16, 36, *36*
volunteers, 20

wigs, 41

X-rays, 25, 40, *40*